BALENCIAGA

KUBLIN

ANA BALDA
MARIA KUBLIN

BALENCIAGA – KUBLIN

A FASHION RECORD
with 163 illustrations

CONTENTS

It was January 2019 when I reached out to Ana Balda for the first time. I had read her PhD thesis on Cristóbal Balenciaga and his relationship with the media, and I was especially interested in the text she had written about my father, fashion photographer and filmmaker Tom Kublin, and his work for the house of Balenciaga. After our initial contact, we started a conversation that went on to become the touring exhibition 'Tom Kublin for Balenciaga: An Unusual Collaboration', inaugurated at the Cristóbal Balenciaga Museum in 2022. The exhibition was based on the creative relationship between two artists: Tom Kublin and Cristóbal Balenciaga.

I am a posthumous child and what I know about my father comes from secondary sources. The most important source is my mother, Katinka, a leading fashion model and my father's muse. To this day I am captivated by the story of their first encounter during a go-see at The Pierre, a hotel on the Upper East Side in New York. '*Un coup de foudre*' was how she described it. A few months later they met again, when my father booked her for their first shoot. From that moment onwards they began working together – creating art together, as she calls it – and eventually developed a relationship.

I had the privilege to spend my childhood surrounded by beautiful art and photography in cosmopolitan cities like Zurich, Milan and Paris. This early exposure made my choice to study history of art a logical one, and specializing in photography came organically. My interest in fashion photography grew gradually and it was only then that I began to research the body of work by my father. Going through his oeuvre, I discovered that he had a signature aesthetic that is best described as refined and elegant minimalism, or understated glamour, a style also favoured by the Spanish couturier Cristóbal Balenciaga. The sizzling synergy between the couturier and the photographer is present throughout the visual material, which in my humble opinion represents one of the most creative unions in fashion history.

Stardom seemed assured, until tragedy struck. At the age of forty-two, whilst on holiday with my mother, Tom Kublin passed away unexpectedly. Although his iconic photographs, which capture the zeitgeist masterfully, are recognized, I believe his premature death is the reason why his name has been somewhat forgotten. The other thing is that he lived and died before the age of celebrity. My goal is to give my father the recognition he deserves; co-curating the exhibition at the Cristóbal Balenciaga Museum was a key moment. The making of this book is another pivotal event. This book presents a great selection of Tom Kublin's work and shows his contribution to fashion photography, and its creation has been very important on so many levels. In-depth research and talking with people who knew and worked with my father have given me such valuable insights into both his personality and work ethic. Through this journey I feel as if I have come closer to knowing him, and for that I am forever grateful.

I first came across Ana Balda and Maria Kublin's exhibition project 'Tom Kublin for Balenciaga: An Unusual Collaboration' in October 2019. The team in charge of programming at the Cristóbal Balenciaga Museum felt that it was a timely proposal that tied in well with our mission.

The Cristóbal Balenciaga Museum opened its doors on 11 June 2011 in the Basque coastal town of Getaria (Gipuzkoa), where the master of haute couture was born on 21 January 1895 and also where he was buried after his death on 24 March 1972. It is an initiative of four public bodies: the Ministry of Culture, the Basque Government, the Provincial Council of Gipuzkoa and the Getaria Town Council. Located in a bespoke architectural building covering 9000 square metres, the museum is set in a rural fishing village with fewer than 3000 inhabitants, where the steep streets, sheltered port and monumental church have barely changed since the days of Cristóbal Balenciaga's childhood. As an independent institution, the museum relies not on the designer's personal archives but on donations and contributions from former clients and collaborators. The collection is now home to more than 3500 specimens with a wide-ranging chronology, including a number of pieces from the early years of Balenciaga's career. Besides protecting this rich heritage, the mission of the museum is to promote research into this global figure and his work and to highlight the importance of his legacy.

A major part of this research and knowledge transfer is carried out through the museum's programme of fashion exhibitions, which fall into two mutually complementary categories. First, there are events that showcase original Balenciaga designs, usually from the in-house collection, in large-format themed exhibitions that are updated annually. The second category is of a more diverse nature, exploring specific aspects of the designer's work and the art of haute couture in a series of temporary mid-scale exhibitions on shorter cycles. Relatively often, this programme of events includes photographic exhibitions. Indeed, fashion photography provides the perfect perspective to accompany and complement the museum's collection, depicting the dressed body and supplying the necessary references and cultural and historic context for visitors to understand fully this designer's work. Furthermore, as a creative discipline, photography has the power to make an impact and create visual associations that remain inextricably linked with the couture creations. With this in mind, the proposal for the 'Tom Kublin for Balenciaga: An Unusual Collaboration' exhibition offered a welcome complementary perspective and an opportunity to look back at the iconography associated with Balenciaga's work.

The exhibition also introduced Tom Kublin to a wider audience. Though the name is already familiar to Cristóbal Balenciaga's community of followers and experts, who know Kublin as the man behind many of the images featured in books, catalogues and exhibitions dedicated to the couturier, the biography and career of this photographer is virtually unknown. The opportunity to reveal who Kublin was, how his career progressed and the nature of his collaboration with Balenciaga, was fascinating new territory. All the more so since these images communicate not only the photographer's gaze but also a perspective on Balenciaga as an internationally acclaimed designer. The exhibition was therefore the perfect fit for the museum's objective of blazing a trail and adding to the knowledge of Balenciaga's universe.

The project was innovative and deserved to be shown, but it did pose one particular problem. When the curators took a closer look at the material, they realised that there were very few negatives and original prints of Kublin's work. For photography purists, this lack of original elements would have been reason enough to rule out the proposal. On the other hand, the material presented did include a considerable number of photographs from old issues of fashion magazines, for instance, *Harper's Bazaar* and *Jardin des Modes,* along with archival images from the Abraham collection at the Swiss National Museum and the Museum of Design Zurich. All in all, more than 100 photographs of Balenciaga's designs were available to exhibit – a considerable body of work that would have remained undiscovered if the project had failed to come to fruition.

Ultimately, the objective of knowledge transfer was prioritized. The concept devised in cooperation with Ciszak Dalmas design studio meant that the primary sources were displayed on the images, providing a visual solution to compensate for the use of digital images.

The exhibition also included footage of Balenciaga's collections from films taken by the photographer between 1963 and 1966. This material, which is vital for understanding Balenciaga's style and his view of elegance, shows models strutting along, turning around, taking off coats and jackets. The excerpts had been shown on previous occasions, with Kublin discreetly credited in the background. But in this setting, Kublin's films were projected from his own standpoint behind the lens, attesting to his evolution as a fashion filmmaker in his work for Balenciaga.

Also among the exhibits was a two-minute film by Kublin which shows Cristóbal Balenciaga putting the finishing touches to his summer 1966 collection before its launch. The footage reveals the sheer focus of the couturier at work and his interactions with the team, at a time when his nerves and stress levels must have been pushed to the limit. It was included to highlight Kublin's important contribution to the house of Balenciaga, not only in terms of ensuring its commercial success but also for helping to document its history.

Finally, the exhibition featured the first-ever projection of the perfume commercial for *Le Dix de Balenciaga*, filmed by Kublin in 1965. This material, found in a badly damaged roll of Super 8 film, was restored and digitized by the museum as a commercial artefact and a deserving part of the couturier's documentary heritage.

For all these reasons it seems apt to say that the Tom Kublin exhibition – open to the public between June and October 2022 – helped to lay the groundwork for future investigations. I believe this book, which builds on the work of the exhibition, will serve as a key reference not only for researchers of Tom Kublin and Balenciaga, but for students of twentieth-century haute couture and fashion photography in general.

TOM KUBLIN & CRISTÓBAL BALENCIAGA

ANA BALDA

Tamás Kublin – known as Thomas Kublin, or Tom – was born on 4 March 1924 in the Hungarian town of Zalaszentgrót. He had a middle-class upbringing, but his father, Jëno Janos Imre Kublin, worked in a lavish palace owned by the aristocratic Esterházy family. The palace was known as the Hungarian Versailles, not only for its architecture but also because it was home to a vast number of artworks.[1] Tom played there from time to time as a young boy, his first brush with the world of art and luxury he would later come to love. At the age of only thirteen, and against his parents' wishes, he was already harbouring ambitions of becoming a photographer. His parents did not take him seriously at first, at least not until the day they realised their son had turned the bathroom into a darkroom for developing his photos. Two years later, they allowed Tom to enrol at the Budapest School of Photography. No one knows where Tom's remarkably early interest in photography came from, but it's true that among the leading photographers of the 1920s and 1930s, there was a significant number of Hungarian names. Gyula Halász (known as Brassaï), André Kertész, László Moholy-Nagy, Martin Munkácsi and Lucien Hervé are some of the photographers who started out in their native Hungary but went on to develop their careers outside of the country, due to war or economic crisis. Tom Kublin would have a similar story.

At the end of the 1930s, photography was present in Hungarian cultural life through the illustrated magazines that published a variety of inspiring images, from aerial views of distant places to portraits of Hollywood stars, to artistic visions of everyday objects in the New Photography style, promoted by Moholy-Nagy and his disciples from the Bauhaus. By the early 1940s, Tom Kublin was already a respected photographer and had established himself within this Budapest scene. In March 1944, one of his still-life photographs was published in the photography journal *Fotoélet*.[2] He also worked on graphic design projects for various magazines, including a cover design for *Fotoriport* in 1943.

Tom Kublin served in the Hungarian army as an official photographer during the final years of the Second World War. Between October 1944 and February 1945, Budapest suffered constant and devastating bombings by Soviet forces who sought to free the city from German rule, claiming it as their own. As a result, the government launched a damage assessment project and commissioned photographers to record the substantial destruction of the historic city, the former seat of the Austro-Hungarian empire. Tom Kublin was one of them.[3] His photographs caught the eye of an American journalist, who was impressed by the quality of Kublin's work and invited him to collaborate on a report which took them to various European cities. The final destination on this trip was Switzerland, where Kublin chose to remain because the future in Budapest was looking uncertain following the Soviet invasion in Hungary.

Tom Kublin opened a photography studio in Zurich and began working on various advertising projects. According to an article in *Harper's Bazaar*, Kublin decided to pursue fashion photography when he was commissioned by a Swiss publication to cover a fashion show in St. Moritz for the French couturier Jacques Fath.[4] The exact date of this event is unrecorded, but it is known that Fath held shows in the Swiss town in 1947 and 1948.[5] In any case, the story goes that during this assignment Kublin's eyes were opened to the possibilities of fashion photography, and, as a result, he decided to devote his career to it.

Kublin opened another studio in Paris in 1951, where he began to work on advertising campaigns and promotional material for fashion brands and the specialist press.[6] Of these early projects, his stand-out photographs were completed on assignment for Hermès and the French women's magazine *Jardin des Modes*.[7] Other publications such as *Town & Country* and *Ladies' Home*

Kublin's Early Life in Hungary

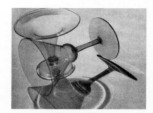

Still life by Tom Kublin in *Fotoélet*, 1944.

Cover design by Tom Kublin, 1943.

Photograph by Tom Kublin of the Royal Palace of Budapest after Soviet bombings, 1945.

Launching a Career in Fashion Photography

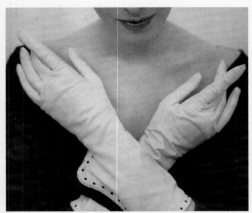

Hermès, pair of women's white leather gloves embroidered and fringed with black silk. Photograph by Tom Kublin, 1951.

Journal also featured photographs by Tom Kublin during the first half of the 1950s, but it was his work for *Harper's Bazaar* that proved particularly intensive. In 1954 the British edition of the magazine named him as one of the photographers to cover the Paris collections on its behalf.[8] This collaboration extended to the US edition from the end of the 1950s and was instrumental in the development of the German edition.[9] In Switzerland, Kublin's first assignments were published in *Der Bund* newspaper and the magazines *Annabelle* and *Textiles Suisses*.[10] The images were signed 'Matter & Kublin,' suggesting they might have been produced in partnership with another photographer named Matter. From 1953 onwards, the photographs are credited to Kublin alone (apart from one exception in 1954, where this joint signature appears again). Most were published in *Textiles Suisses* and show haute couture designs made from fabrics supplied by the Swiss silk-making company Abraham, based in Zurich. The hub of a thriving textile industry since the nineteenth century, this city was famed for its silk and cotton fabrics.

Kublin and Abraham

Abraham had already been providing Parisian haute couture houses with fabrics since before the Second World War, but when the war ended the company increasingly turned its attention to these houses to cement its status as a luxury fashion supplier.[11] In a bid to expand its client base in this sector, the company's director Gustav Zumsteg set about collecting and preserving press clippings about the company, building a portfolio of samples to showcase the finest fabrics it had produced each season, and compiling a systematic photographic record of Parisian haute couture designs made with its silks.[12] Today, the Abraham Textile Archive is held in the Swiss National Museum, Zurich.

The first photographs for the Abraham portfolio were taken between 1948 and 1953 by photographers including Willy Maywald, André Ostier and Ostier-Heil (André Ostier and Eugene Francis Heil). From 1953, however, the images bear Tom Kublin's signature. He continued to be closely aligned with this Zurich-based textile manufacturer throughout his career; from 1953 until Kublin's death 1966, Abraham commissioned him to photograph hundreds of models from fashion houses ranging from Fath, Rochas and Pierre Balmain to Christian Dior, Givenchy, Lanvin, Chanel, Yves Saint Laurent and, most frequently, Balenciaga.

The remarkable number of designs by Cristóbal Balenciaga that feature in the Abraham Textile Archive – more than 150 – shows that the couturier became a major client for the company from the mid-1950s. The fashion house had been an occasional customer prior to this, but records show that even in 1952, Abraham still had to work hard to sell its fabrics to Balenciaga.[13] Before long, the business relationship was consolidated, and it planted the seed for the professional collaboration between Balenciaga and photographer Tom Kublin.

Postwar Fashion, A New Era

The fashion industry and fashion photography itself were in a period of transformation when Tom Kublin embarked on his project with Abraham. Since the mid-nineteenth century, Parisian haute couture had set the trends for women's fashion, and these were in turn conveyed by the press to readers all over the world, mostly through illustrations and photographs in fashion magazines. In the interwar period, the fashion press gave precedence to images that showcased designs by French couturiers. In a memo to the photographers tasked with taking pictures of haute couture, American *Vogue* editor Edna Woolman Chase demanded: 'Concentrate completely on showing the dress, light it for this purpose and if that can't be done with art then art be damned. *Show the dress*.'[14]

Parisian fashion was the main attraction in fashion magazines, and editors did their best to please the couturiers by choosing photographs that would elevate their designs.

This dynamic began to change after the Second World War, particularly in the 1950s and 1960s as prêt-à-porter – the more affordable option, inspired by the latest trends from Paris – began to take over from haute couture. This shift can be traced through the magazines, as reporting moved away from haute couture in favour of features on mass-produced fashion. Inevitably, the style of photography evolved as result. Elegant, static images taken indoors, free from any excessive elements that might detract from the leading role of the garments, gave way to a new breed of images: here, the focus was on presenting prêt-à-porter in exotic spaces and with striking models.[15] Over time, this phenomenon took the spotlight away from the art of haute couture and the obsession with its technical and innovative capacity that had dominated fashion photography during the earlier twentieth century.[16]

Balenciaga vs the Fashion Press

Cristóbal Balenciaga made his international press debut with the unveiling of his first Paris collection in 1937. *Vogue*, *Harper's Bazaar*, *L'Officiel* and other famous publications showed these first Balenciaga creations to the world in beautiful photographs by Horst P. Horst, George Hoyningen-Huene and Madame d'Ora. Later, after the Second World War, a new cohort of photographers led by Irving Penn and Richard Avedon created historic images of the couturier's designs. By 1955, however, the changes in the fashion industry and the media were already having an adverse effect on Balenciaga and his business. Against this backdrop, the designer began to work with Tom Kublin.

The sale of licences had been an important part of the haute couture business since the mid-nineteenth century. Clothing designs were sold to clients under licence agreements so that they could be replicated and grace the shelves in luxury establishments around the world. This process, however, inevitably led to the rogue trade of illegal copies. To prevent this from happening, and to protect their lawful authorship, Parisian haute couture houses commissioned photographers to record of the collections they launched each year.[17] Balenciaga appointed Kublin to produce images in this category between 1955 and 1966. With at least two collections per year, each comprising more than 200 pieces, Kublin photographed several thousands of designs by Balenciaga.

Cristóbal Balenciaga in his salon at 10 avenue George V, Paris, photograph by Tom Kublin, 1957. Balenciaga Archives Paris

These documentary photographs were taken from various perspectives – generally head-on and from the back, but sometimes also in profile. In most cases, a card with the reference number for the design was displayed at the model's feet as she posed. With a few exceptions, Kublin's models can be seen holding this number in their hands, just as they did when the collections were shown to the fashion press and clients. Balenciaga traded with a number of prestigious establishments from all over the world, particularly the US. Clients of the couture house included Saks Fifth Avenue, Bergdorf Goodman, Macy's, Ohrbach's and Bloomingdale's, all of whom sold replicas of Balenciaga designs manufactured under licence agreements.[18] This allowed American customers to buy original Balenciaga pieces without having to travel to Paris, and at more affordable prices.

Buyers from these major department stores would usually attend the biannual fashion shows in Paris organized by the Chambre Syndicale de la Couture, the umbrella organisation for the most prestigious couture houses. Attendees were forbidden to take photographs or sketch the designs they saw, and the Chambre made the press wait four weeks before publishing images of the collections. This month-long period was intended to give the major department stores enough time to reproduce the designs they had purchased under licence agreements and for the products to reach the shelves. Still, many journalists ignored this rule and proceeded to publish sketches or photographs of the designs immediately after the showings. This material, in the hands of outsiders, created a breeding ground for illicit copies which made their way into stores even faster than the licensed products. Piracy seriously harmed the sale of Parisian haute couture licences, with the most influential houses (Balenciaga included) among the worst hit. While major department stores waited patiently for their lawfully purchased designs to be manufactured, other establishments were already displaying very similar-looking garments in their windows, sometimes even in the same street. And to add insult to injury, at absurdly low prices. This phenomenon put off potential buyers and led to a drop in licence sales.

Feeling completely defenceless in this situation, Balenciaga decided to schedule his own cycle of fashion shows – independent of the Chambre's calendar. From January 1956, he held his own private show for clients four weeks before the collections were revealed to the press. He succeeded in keeping his designs under wraps until the licensed copies were ready for sale in the department stores, but the move inevitably incensed the press. Some media sources believed it interfered with their duty to report on the latest news, saying it made no sense to talk about Balenciaga's designs a whole month after the fact.[19] Moreover, the expectation to travel to Paris twice in such a short period was an additional financial and organizational burden for US journalists.[20] To spare them the effort, the couturier provided images that Kublin had taken of his creations – usually photographs of designs that had been sold under licence and were already gracing window displays.[21] This allowed Balenciaga to protect the licensing side of his business and bolster his buyers' commercial success, while also making life easier for the fashion press. He shared images that had been taken by someone he trusted wholeheartedly and whose work conformed with his idea of photography as a form that should highlight the beauty of haute couture, its technical mastery and innovation.

Despite Balenciaga's conflict with the press the year before, in October 1957, the British edition of *Harper's Bazaar* published an extended piece celebrating the twentieth anniversary of the house of Balenciaga in Paris, which also pictured various creations from his most recent collection.[22] The feature opened with a full-page close-up of Cristóbal Balenciaga, shot by Tom Kublin. The two men continued to be friends and colleagues until Kublin's sudden death on 30 May 1966; many years later, Hubert de Givenchy would refer to Tom Kublin as Balenciaga's favourite photographer.[23]

Avant-Garde Friendships

Back in the early 1950s, Cristóbal Balenciaga and Gustav Zumsteg belonged to the same circle of friends surrounding the art dealers Aimé and Marguerite Maeght, which would soon welcome Tom Kublin into the fold, too.[24] Zumsteg had met the Maeghts in Paris after serving his apprenticeship in the Zurich headquarters; this was at a time when Ludwig Abraham had put him in charge of Soierie ABC Lyons, a French subsidiary of the Swiss company.[25] The Maeghts, who represented a number of French avant-garde artists, introduced Zumsteg to Braque, Léger, Chagall, Miró, Giacometti and others, and these connections were instrumental in the major art collection he built up over the years. Part of this collection adorned the walls of the prestigious Kronenhalle restaurant in Zurich, which was owned by Zumsteg's mother and where he often entertained his acquaintances from the art and fashion worlds. Balenciaga often called at the Kronenhalle on his visits to the Swiss city. Other famous names from Parisian haute couture also frequented the restaurant, including Gabrielle Chanel and Yves Saint Laurent, who were also among Abraham's valued customers.[26] Tom Kublin was another regular at the Kronenhalle. His former assistant Gian Paolo Barbieri remembers attending the restaurant for the tribute that Zumsteg organized in Kublin's honour when he died.[27]

LEFT Marc Chagall, photograph by Tom Kublin for *Harper's Bazaar*, 1959. RIGHT Cristóbal Balenciaga in his home study, avenue Marceau, Paris, photograph by Cecil Beaton, 1956.

Being part of this circle cultivated Kublin's interest in the art world. Though he wasn't a collector in the strict sense, like his friend Zumsteg, the various art books he amassed, along with lithographs by Picasso, Matisse, Chagall and Miró, a few Picasso linocuts and a pochoir by the illustrator George Barbier, speak to this photographer's love of the arts. These ties to the art scene gave Kublin the opportunity to portray some of the artists he most admired, including Giacometti, Calder, Miró and Van Dongen.[28] *Harper's Bazaar* published a number of these portraits, most notably his full-page close-up of Marc Chagall, which was taken to celebrate the retrospective exhibition of the Russian-French artist's work at the Musée des Arts Décoratifs in 1959.[29] But this wasn't Kublin's only portrait of Chagall; in the 1956 photograph of Balenciaga by Cecil Beaton, the photograph beside the couturier depicts Marc Chagall in his studio and was also taken by Tom Kublin.[30]

Tom Kublin was not only inspired by other artists, but he was also a keen draughtsman. According to an article in *Women's Wear Daily*, he even designed some prints for Abraham.[31] Kublin would draw his ideas in advance of his photography shoots. The pages from his sketchbook in the lead-up to photoshoots for the Spring/Summer 1961 haute couture collections show him working out various elements, such as the positioning of the models, the kinds of lighting he wanted to use and the desired qualities of the set. The notes next to the sketches include repeated references to master painters including Goya, Velázquez and Bellini, as well as to modern artists like Mondrian and Chagall. These artists gave Kublin inspiration, informing his use of light and helping him to create suitable backdrops to elevate the models in the designer's haute couture creations.

LEFT Giovanni Bellini, *Madonna and Child,* 1480s; RIGHT Tom Kublin's sketchbook for the S/S 1961 haute couture collections; BELOW Tom Kublin for *Town & Country*, 1961.

One sketch (see right) depicts two lamp shades and records the desired wattage for each. In the background between the lamp shades is a large rectangle with the note 'high grey,' and inside this is a narrower rectangle that has been shaded in pencil and marked 'Dunkel Grau' (dark grey). The darker hatched section at the bottom of the sketch reads 'Schwarz' (black). Underneath, towards the corner, one can just about make out the words 'abstracte Bellini', almost like a title for the scene he is picturing. Painting in the late fifteenth century, Giovanni Bellini often played with linear perspective: he would draw a landscape in the background, then paint a large rectangle on top in vibrant colours and use it as the backdrop for his Madonna paintings. The April 1961 issue of *Town & Country* contains a piece about the Spring/Summer collections from Paris with photographs by Kublin.[32] This feature is most likely one of the projects the photographer was preparing for in his workbook; here we see that he has dispensed with the landscape from Bellini's backdrops, opting instead for a grey background with a superimposed narrower rectangle in intense grey, the model positioned at the front of the set to enhance the sense of perspective. The lighter floor helps to intensify the effect.

In 1958, when Tom Kublin was working on an extensive series of photographs for Parisian haute couture designers (mostly Cristóbal Balenciaga) he chose for the backdrop a large, opulent curtain – a technique used by Renaissance and Baroque painters to make the subject appear more distinguished. Velázquez, Rubens and other master painters often depicted princes and cardinals posing in front of rich, voluminous drapery. According to the late Willie Landels, the first editor of *Harper's & Queen* magazine and an acquaintance of Kublin's, the inspiration for this particular photographic series came from Leonardo da Vinci's drapery studies.[33] In one of the photographs, a model poses in front of the curtain, wearing a design referred to by the magazine as a 'petal' dress because of its resemblance to a flower.[34] The model's body tilts slightly towards a large antique stand on which a small painting is displayed. Kublin introduced this element into the set, positioning it as if it were a mirror, when in fact it is a copy of *Portrait of a Young Girl* (*c.* 1470) by the Flemish master Petrus Christus.[35] The model's hair, styled by Christian,

LEFT Leonardo da Vinci, *Drapery for a Seated Figure, c.* 1470. RIGHT Tom Kublin for *Harper's Bazaar* UK, 1958.

LEFT Edgar Degas, *Dancer Putting on Her Shoes*, c. 1880–85. RIGHT Antoinette Sibley, photograph by Tom Kublin for *Harper's Bazaar* UK, 1959.

a hairdresser who collaborated with Balenciaga many times, is in an updo with added volume at the top of her head, emulating the lines of the headdress worn by the girl in the painting. Regarded as the first painting to show the close-up of a human figure with perspective – a technique which Christus had learned in Italy, at a time when perspective had recently been incorporated into landscape painting – this work of art occupies a special place in the portrait genre. Kublin possibly came across the copy in an antique shop, or perhaps it belonged to one of the collectors he knew through the Maeghts – maybe he even borrowed it from Balenciaga himself, given the designer's fondness for browsing antique shops. The unique nature of the painting may have prompted Kublin to incorporate it into this series of photographs, where the influence of art history is clear to see.

Kublin's collection of art books and prints was also a source of inspiration. When the British edition of *Harper's Bazaar* published a piece on artists from the London scene in 1959, it opened with a photograph by Kublin of the ballerina Antoinette Sibley – an image that bears a striking resemblance to a painting of a dancer by Edgar Degas,[36] featured in a book in Kublin's personal collection. There are also stylistic similarities between a Picasso linocut that Kublin kept among his art prints and the photographs he took to illustrate a report on the latest hair trends, published in *Harper's Bazaar*, June 1954.

Did these artistic influences help to cement a photographic style? And what about other photographers; did they influence him too? Is there such thing as a Tom Kublin style?

A Distinctive Photographic Style

Kublin was a fan of Alfred Stieglitz and particularly liked his photograph *The Steerage* (1907). He was also fond of André Kertész, especially his *Satiric Dancer* (1926).[37] Given that Kublin attended the School of Photography in Budapest, it is fair to assume he was at least familiar with Stieglitz – regarded as the father of photography as an artform – and his *Camera Work* project. Indeed, Kublin's close-up view of the overturned truck in Budapest after the Soviet bombings bears many similarities with the close-up of the gangway in *The Steerage*. We can also assume that he was acquainted with the work of fellow Hungarian Kertész, whose work was being published in Hungarian photography magazines while Kublin was a student. The still-life by Kublin featured in the photography journal *Fotoélet* in 1944 is evocative not only of Kertész but also speaks to the influence of the photographs from the New Vision movement, with their surprising framings and plays of light.

Notwithstanding these early influences, Kublin began to develop his own style when he specialized as a fashion photographer. Richard Avedon had pioneered a fresh, innovative approach to fashion photography in the 1940s; with his photographs for *Harper's Bazaar,* he served as the successor to Martin Munkácsi and his action photography. Avedon's outdoor photographs of smiling, vivacious models dressed in glamorous haute couture creations were a cinematographic story that filled postwar readers with inspiration. Kublin experimented with outdoor photography, for example in his first advertising campaign for Hermès and in his early work for *Harper's Bazaar*. But he was quick to realise that natural light was an uncontrollable variable and decided that he preferred studio photography instead.[38] The fast-paced nature of the haute couture industry also factored in to his choice: the reports often had to be finished in less than twenty-four hours to make sure they were ready for the buyers, which meant that more often than not the team would have to work at night time. Whatever the reason, Tom Kublin was a studio photographer. Other major lensmen in this category included Irving Penn, Cecil Beaton and Horst P. Horst. But they all worked primarily for *Vogue*, leaving an opening for Tom Kublin and his studio photography in *Harper's Bazaar*, which attracted contributions from renowned photographers including

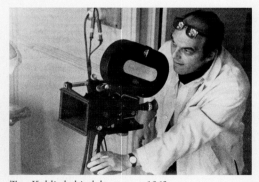

Tom Kublin behind the camera, 1965.

the aforementioned Richard Avedon, Louise Dahl-Wolfe and Tony Frissell, who specialized not in studio photography but dealt primarily with moving subjects and natural light.

It is tempting to compare Tom Kublin to Irving Penn, Cecil Beaton and Horst P. Horst. Indeed, it is true that his peers all photographed models in static poses in indoor environments. However, while Irving Penn viewed fashion as if it were a still-life object, dispensing with any element that might interfere with the main attraction, Kublin tended to use additional tools to emphasize the notions of elegance, innovation or exclusivity in the piece. For example, the 1958 photograph in which Kublin placed Petrus Christus's painting on an antique stand against the backdrop of a sumptuous curtain (see p. 17) situates Balenciaga's petal dress in the art historical tradition and makes the design appear unique, exclusive and timeless, like good art. And on the occasions when Kublin opted for a smooth grey backdrop, his gaze was sharper and less pictorial than that of Penn.

Kublin's work does not have much in common with Cecil Beaton's photography, either. The English photographer used the set to excessive, theatrical, baroque effect, and his inclusion of flowers, candles, lace, and furniture spoke of an aristocratic, luxurious lifestyle that remained out of reach for most. Horst P. Horst's photographs often featured architectural elements, such as columns, with pure lines, to convey a refined and minimalist concept of elegance. When Tom Kublin chose a particular element for his mise-en-scène, however, he did so solely to express the image of the fashion label at the heart of the photograph.

LEFT TO RIGHT Tom Kublin; the hairdresser Christian; and Ramón Esparza, Cristóbal Balenciaga's right-hand man, 1958.

Many of Kublin's photographs for Balenciaga were taken inside its Parisian headquarters – a grand nineteenth-century townhouse at 10 avenue George V – incorporating furniture from the salon or the tile flooring from the boutique. Most of the photographs of models in the parlours also feature traditional gilded wood chairs (see for example pp. 55, 69), sometimes strewn about the space after the style of Kertész's famous *Chairs, Champs Elysées*. These chairs were commonly found in haute couture houses and, at a time when couture imitations were ubiquitous, Kublin used them to locate his models in the house of Balenciaga and to communicate that these were truly original designs.

Tom Kublin behind the camera, 1966.

The body of work that Tom Kublin produced for Balenciaga over the years exudes a kind of restrained elegance that is reminiscent of the school of fashion photography pioneered by Edward Steichen at *Vogue* in the 1920s. These were the photographs that shaped Cristóbal Balenciaga's visual world in the early days of his haute couture house in San Sebastián, when he was working on his technique in a bid to emulate Vionnet and Chanel, both designers he admired.[39] It is clear that when Balenciaga met Tom Kublin, he found someone who could contextualize his creations in the photographic tradition of the classic, elegant gaze of haute couture. The photographs in this book perfectly demonstrate that in Tom Kublin, Cristóbal Balenciaga had discovered an exceptional ally who would champion his identity as the quintessential, timeless couturier. The photos also show that the opulent curtain, the chairs in the showing parlour, and even the numbers in the hands of the models in the archival photographs, were more than simple props; they were Tom Kublin's contribution to creating a unique Balenciaga iconography that has stood the test of time.

Tom Kublin recorded films of Balenciaga's collections from the start of the 1960s until 1966, usually on an Arriflex 35 camera. His evolution as a fashion filmmaker during this period is clear to see. The earliest films (see for example pp. 133–34) were shot in black and white and in real time, on a static camera which he positioned at a slight angle from the catwalk, capturing the models as they strutted out towards the lens. We see the models emerging and walking head-on towards the camera, then turning around and returning to the start. The viewing angle shows the garments in some detail from three perspectives: from the front, the back and in profile. The footage gives us unparalleled

Films for Balenciaga

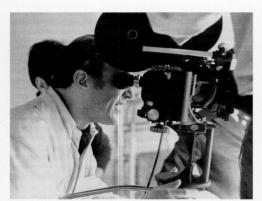
Tom Kublin behind the camera, 1966.

Tom Kublin and Katinka at their apartment in Zurich, 1965.

insights into Balenciaga's concept of fashion beyond the aesthetic of his designs. By watching the way the models walk and move, how they take off their coats, jackets and trench coats, we gain a better understanding of Cristóbal Balenciaga's idea of elegance.

Kublin began to edit his films as of the Autumn/Winter 1964–65 collection, cutting short each model's catwalk appearance. From this point on, the footage is no longer in real time. At the beginning and the end of the films, he also incorporated close-ups of beautiful models wearing hats and hair accessories (see p. 151). And whereas Balenciaga showed his collections to audiences in complete silence, Kublin introduced music to enhance the viewing experience.

Kublin continued to add new touches to subsequent films, making them even shorter than before. For the Autumn/Winter 1965–66 collection, instead of filming the models during the client showings, he made them walk for the camera alone. He incorporated various close-ups, panning the camera up and down the garments to highlight their aesthetic and technical qualities. His final films were shot in colour and introduced choreography, showing several models in the same sequence, turning and spinning around one another (see pp. 174–75). With all these changes, Kublin's films were no longer simple archival footage; they were beginning to resemble commercials. The mid-1960s was a time of crisis for haute couture. This crisis also affected Balenciaga, who was suffering from the increasing lack of licence buyers for his private shows. It is likely that the designer commissioned these films as a way of boosting this line of business without making his clients to travel to Paris; some of the couture designs in the films can be seen in photos of fashion shows held in prestigious US stores, such as Bloomingdale's and Ohrbach's.[40] Another film on this list is Kublin's 1965 commercial for Balenciaga's perfumes (see p. 167). Kublin chose his partner and muse Katinka Bleeker, whom he had met in New York in 1963, as the model for this assignment, with Paris providing the backdrop.[41]

The most valuable footage Tom Kublin ever recorded, however, is his film of Cristóbal Balenciaga behind the scenes at the Spring/Summer 1966 show, working against the clock with his team as they make the very final touches (see pp. 180–84). Given that Kublin worked on this film not long before his death, it was probably one of his final assignments for the fashion house. Around this same time, when fashion had made it onto the small screen, Kublin filmed an advertisement for the cosmetic brand Coty and he was also busy filming a 30-minute colour documentary on fashion trends for US television, which was intended to showcase everything from 'fabrics to hairdos, through makeup and haute couture', but sadly never saw the light of day.[42]

A Fashion Legacy

Tom Kublin, photograph by Jack Nisberg, c. 1950–66.

Tom Kublin died suddenly of a stroke on 30 May 1966 while on a break with Katinka in Locarno, Switzerland. Although the photographer was only forty-two years old, his output had been prolific. He had continued to produce work for the fashion press, Balenciaga and Abraham until he died.[43] Kublin also photographed a number of famous faces of the era, most notably actress Elizabeth Taylor, couturiers Cristóbal Balenciaga and Yves Saint Laurent, ballerina Margot Fontaine, and the artists Kees van Dongen, Joan Miró, Alexander Calder and, as already noted, Marc Chagall.[44] Kublin appointed assistants to help carry out his broad-ranging, productive activities: names that would later excel in their chosen fields, including the Italian fashion photographer Gian Paolo Barbieri, known for the photographs he produced for Valentino's first campaigns, and the Swiss filmmaker Moritz de Hadeln, who later became the director of the Berlin and Venice international film festivals.[45]

As well as providing essential material for research into haute couture in the 1950s and 1960s – the era historians call the 'golden age' of fashion – Tom Kublin's body of photographic and filmic work is a valuable legacy, an inspiration for photographers working in the field.

CONVERSATION WITH KATINKA

MARIA KUBLIN

It's a sunny December afternoon when I am preparing for the interview with my mother, former Miss Holland, supermodel, stylist and photographer Katinka Bleeker. The mood is serene and relaxed and I know that we both are looking forward to this. In fact, it feels rather special interviewing a woman whose life reads like a novel. At the age of 17 she left Amsterdam to pursue a successful modelling career in New York. Seven years later, she had a meeting that would change her life for ever. This meeting was with the influential fashion photographer, filmmaker and the man who would become my father, Tom Kublin.

How did you meet Tom Kublin?

It was 1963, New York, and I was a 24-year-old top model on the books with Eileen Ford's model agency, making $60 an hour (equivalent to $585 today). I lived at the famous Barbizon Hotel for well-to-do women and women who were on the brink of a career breakthrough. The Barbizon residents list reads like a who's-who of Hollywood and literary royalty. Grace Kelly, Liza Minelli, Joan Crawford and literary stars Sylvia Plath and Joan Didion were amongst the household names who arrived as young unknowns. One day, my model agency made a go-see appointment with Tom Kublin at the Pierre Hotel, on the Upper East Side. Little did I know that this meeting would change my life for good, and that I would become Tom's fiancée and muse. Being a model, I had met and worked with many image-makers, from Richard Avedon to Hiro, but this time was different. I experienced a *coup de foudre* during my first meeting with Tom. There was something about his mannerisms that I thought was quite unique and is best described as old-fashioned charm. After flicking through the pages of my portfolio, Tom thanked me for my time and that was that. Subconsciously, I was sure that he would book me for the shoot, but nothing happened. Later, in Paris, my agent Dorian Leigh, a former model and sister of the model Suzy Parker, told me to meet Tom Kublin again for another go-see appointment. I was reluctant because he did not book me in New York, so why would he book me now? Dorian Leigh convinced me to go. As a former model herself, she knew that a model could be rejected for one shoot, but be perfect for another assignment. So I went, and from that moment on we were a couple. Our private and professional lives were very entwined, and the foundation of our life together was built on creativity.

What inspired Kublin's work? How did he prepare for his photographic sessions?

From an early age, Tom was surrounded with lavish beauty. He had a privileged childhood, growing up spending time in the grand environment of the Esterházy family estate and its Rococo and Baroque palace, where his father worked. This experience left a big impression on Tom and formed the basis of his quest for beauty throughout his career. It is remarkable that both Balenciaga and Kublin were acquainted with royalty, and all that comes with it, at a young age. Tom had admiration for the arts in all forms: theatre, ballet and classical music concerts. Tom also had a great respect and admiration for painters and acknowledged that he was inspired by great works of art, visiting museums on a regular basis. He also cultivated lifelong friendships with Chagall, Matisse, Miró and Picasso, who inspired his work. Regarding his working routine, Tom was a perfectionist by nature, and he prepared by making sketches before a shoot. Drawing preliminary sketches was a way to decide how to position the model, props and lighting. Tom used a large-format (10" × 8") single-sheet camera that would give high resolution and depth of field. During a shoot, hushed tones prevailed. Tom was strung up, and he asked full commitment of his two assistants and everybody else on set.

Did Kublin particularly admire the work of any other photographers or artists?
Tom admired Alfred Stieglitz, especially *The Steerage* (1907), as well as *Satiric Dancer* (1926) by fellow Hungarian photographer, André Kertész. He loved the work of Martin Munkácsi, another Hungarian photographer. Tom was also inspired by artists like Matisse and Chagall, and by Old Masters like Zurbarán (whose works were introduced to him by Balenciaga) and Da Vinci. It was not just the visual arts that were sources of inspiration for Tom. He was fascinated by Stravinsky's groundbreaking piece *The Rite of Spring* (1913), and at home we often played music by Beethoven.

Have you ever met Gustav Zumsteg [director of the Swiss silk-making company Abraham]? Did he ever speak about Balenciaga?
I have met him a few times. He was charming and of course a true artist with fabrics. He always spoke with respect about Balenciaga. Zumsteg played an important role in Tom's career: he eased him into the world of haute couture by introducing him to Balenciaga. Zumsteg also introduced Tom to his artist friends, with whom Tom mingled because he loved the artistic environment. In fact, Tom was frequently inspired by art and bought works of art, like the Degas portfolio.

What was the relationship between Kublin and Balenciaga? Did Kublin work exclusively for Balenciaga or did he take photographs for any other fashion designers?
Kublin and Balenciaga had a mutual understanding. I believe this was because they had so much in common: as I mentioned earlier, both were introduced to royalty and grandeur whilst growing up; both knew at a very young age which careers they wanted to pursue; they lost their fathers at an early age; and they both fled their homelands due to war and lived in exile. Furthermore, both men were perfectionists and would go the extra mile to achieve this. Tom's association with Balenciaga, collaborating for more than a decade, created a visual dialogue in the process. I remember Tom telling me that he learned from Balenciaga, and Balenciaga learned from him too. Looking at Tom's photographs gave Balenciaga the opportunity to see his designs from a different perspective. As a freelance photographer, Tom worked mostly for Balenciaga, but also produced work for Christian Dior, Hubert de Givenchy and Yves Saint Laurent, among others.

Who else was involved with Kublin's photoshoots?
Tom liked to work with the same people. With hairdressers Christian and Alexandre, for example: they were a coherent team.

Did Balenciaga attend the photoshoots with Kublin? Did he offer advice or direction on how the photographs should look, for example the way the models should pose, the backdrops?
Balenciaga didn't attend photoshoots. As far as I know Balenciaga trusted Tom completely, and therefore did not feel the need to be there during shoots. It was a collaboration with clear designated roles: Balenciaga focused on his designs, and Kublin used his artistic creativity to make the designs look stunning. Also, Balenciaga often worked 18-hour days and simply did not have time to visit the set. Because Balenciaga was not present,

Tom had total creative freedom. He chose the models and instructed them how to pose. Balenciaga is known for surrounding himself with professionals, and Tom was a professional. Tom would spend hours on one shot, the composition, adjusting the lighting and so on. He was such an expert in making sure the garments received the justice they deserved, whilst communicating the essence of Balenciaga. Balenciaga knew this, and so he felt comfortable to leave the shoots to Tom.

Did Kublin ever feel restricted when working for Balenciaga?
Tom never said anything about feeling restricted. However, there is a big difference between his work for Balenciaga editorials, where he had complete artistic freedom, and the rather formal photographs of the garments that were taken for documentation purposes. Having worked with Tom, I know he preferred the 'artistic' photographs, because they challenged him and brought out his creative ideas.

Were Balenciaga and Kublin friends or was their relationship strictly professional?
They were friends, but I remember that it was always a 'big thing' when Tom was invited to have dinner with Balenciaga. It was always special to be invited by Balenciaga. But I have never met him.

Most of the photos by Kublin for Balenciaga were taken indoors, do you know why?
Firstly, to avoid distractions, Tom preferred to work in his Paris studio, where he had total reign. He always prepared in advance, and he would sketch out where he would like the model to stand and the positioning of props. He mainly used fixed lighting and no flash. Secondly, most of the time the shoots took place at night, because during the day the garments needed to be available for clients to view.

Did Kublin take photos outdoors when working for other fashion designers or magazines?
Tom did some outdoor shoots for *Harper's*. In fact, we did one together in the South of France. Although he was pleased with the results, he preferred working in the studio.

It seems that Kublin's photographs were mainly published in Harper's Bazaar, *especially the British edition. Do you know why? Did he have an exclusivity contract with this magazine?*
It is true that he primarily worked for *Harper's Bazaar*. Tom Kublin was a freelance fashion photographer, therefore I can't imagine he signed any kind of exclusivity contract with *Harper's*. He worked foremost for *Harper's* UK, but he liked New York and always spoke fondly about Diana Vreeland, then editor-in-chief of *Harper's Bazaar* US, and he also had a good rapport with Alexey Brodovitch, the magazine's art director, with whom he talked a lot about work.

What were Kublin's acceptance criteria for his photographs?
During shoots, Tom gave me instructions on how to pose. This could take hours as the changes in poses were very subtle. Once he knew he had 'the' shot, we were finished. In the darkroom, Tom knew which image was the right one. It is difficult to explain what his criteria were, other than that he knew when the photograph was good. It was his intuition.

In your opinion, is there a distinctive Tom Kublin style that can be seen in his photographs for Balenciaga and in his other work?
Going through his body of work, one can see that Tom had a certain style: simple, uncluttered but quietly romantic, a style that the art curator Martin Harrison would hail as 'quietly distinguished'. Therefore, I believe you know a Tom Kublin when you see one.

One day, Tom asked me if I could create a Chagall-like atmosphere because the Dior collection had been inspired by Chagall. That morning, when I'd finished my rounds, I went to the flower market and bought gladioli and mimosa. In a grocery store I gathered about 50 different jars and filled them with paint in Chagall's colours, and then I set up a big table, spattering it with all the paint and filling the jars with flowers. I was fortunate because I knew the photos of Chagall's studio on the French Riviera by heart. Tom arrived just as I was finishing up, and stopped at the door. He was spellbound. He said, 'I wasn't expecting that from you.' When the collections were over, he paid me a wonderful compliment, saying that he'd never had an assistant like me. This internship really opened the doors of the fashion world for me.

Tom was very demanding. If we so much as creased the sheets of paper we were using as a backdrop, we had to redo the whole thing at our own expense. He used very little light. The light sources were almost always lampshades covered with black fabric. He didn't allow the model to move until he'd found the right lighting. I once saw a model cry because her shoes were so tight but she couldn't move. He loved the work of Braque, Velázquez, Goya. He gave me a book about Braque, which I still fondly possess. But it all ended when he died of a stroke. The funeral was in Zurich; Balenciaga attended and I went with Gustav, who held a memorial lunch at his restaurant Kronenhalle. I picked a white rose out of one of the many vases of flowers and laid it on his grave. I owe a great deal to Tom.

TOM KUBLIN & HARPER'S BAZAAR

LYDIA SLATER

Kublin (he was always credited in its pages by his surname) began working at *Harper's Bazaar* in London at a pivotal time for the magazine. During the Second World War, and for several years afterwards, *Harper's Bazaar* in Britain had had to rethink its position as a style title, especially with clothes rationing in force, and the reader herself no longer a lady of leisure but an active participant in the war effort. The magazine's focus had therefore moved away from society and haute couture: instead, its pages during wartime had been filled with articles on food (an understandable preoccupation), and serialized fiction. Meanwhile, fashion photography itself was in short supply. During the war, the photographs in the UK edition were primarily taken by Nancy Sandys Walker, Norman Parkinson's former assistant, while the covers could no longer be photographed in America and the plates shipped across the Atlantic, because of the threat from German U-boats. Instead, the covers were drawn by European-based artists such as Frederic Henrion. So in 1951, when Eileen Dickson, formerly *Bazaar's* fashion editor, took the helm of the magazine, her primary aim was to steer it back into the first flight of fashion. Fortunately, her period of editorship coincided with the lifting of paper rationing, meaning that the page quality drastically improved, and the magazine was able to return to publishing 12 issues a year. Known as the 'Queen of Hats', Dickson, a glamorous blonde, was a byword for chic, always dressed in the latest fashions bought during business trips to America. An early decision she took was to move the magazine's offices to Mayfair, to reflect the image of luxury and glamour she wished it to project. But Dickson's overriding ambition was to broaden *Bazaar's* international clout – and she chose Kublin as part of her armoury.

Kublin first began working for *Bazaar* around the same time that he was recruited to take photographs for the House of Balenciaga's archives. It has been suggested that perhaps Carmel Snow, the editor of American *Bazaar* and a great friend and supporter of Balenciaga's, brokered the introduction. In which case, however, it would seem odd that Kublin only began working for the American edition in 1960, after six fruitful years with *Bazaar* in the UK, and when Snow herself had moved on. His first pictures for the British edition of *Bazaar* appear in the March 1954 issue, which was designed as an international fashion magazine, covering collections in Italy and Spain, Paris and London. Kublin – listed as 'Kubelin', a mistake that was not to reoccur – shot the Italian pictures. In the first, the immaculately groomed model is posed on a Roman hillside. Clad in a white Antonelli gown and long gloves, she holds a posy of flowers and stares impassively at the

camera, looking, in her static elegance, like a latter-day Gibson girl. Another outfit has been shot amid Roman ruins, with the model posed between toppled pediments, framed by towering columns of brick, the lines of which are echoed in the ribbons stitched down the front of her crisp black dress. Despite the dramatic setting, the eye is immediately drawn to the details of the clothing.

The results must have pleased Dickson, since Kublin's work began to proliferate in her pages. The following month, he had the cover, presumably shot during the same trip to Italy. The model stands off-centre, in front of a soft ochre-plastered wall, across which fall the slanting shadows of the window-frames, their geometric shapes subtly echoed in her harlequin-effect shirt and checked hat. For the all-important September fashion issue of the same year, Kublin was chosen to photograph the Paris collections, his pictures accompanied by fashion drawings by the Canadian-born artist Irwin Crosthwait. As with Kublin's first Italian shoot, most of the photographs are taken outside, on location in parks and squares of central Paris. But Kublin also used Crosthwait's abstract paintings to frame two studio shots, one of a Fath ensemble, the other of a scarlet Dior gown – the only image published in colour. Clearly, he himself felt that the studio shots were more impactful than the more natural reportage style of the location pictures; and these were to become his stock-in-trade.

The following month, he was honoured with a short biography in the magazine: 'Thomas Kublin...has, in this past year, done a great deal of beautiful work for *Harper's Bazaar*,' ran the piece, detailing his youthful determination to study photography (setting up a darkroom in his parents' bathroom at the age of 13), and his wartime experiences. As regards his switch to fashion: 'He is mad about it, he says, and thinks of it night and day; he is excited by each job as it comes along, fertile in ideas for presentation and 'props'; he has an equable disposition – there are no scenes – but he is always strung up when he is working; and his best work has a high-key, very romantic quality.' Clearly, Kublin had become as indispensable to the visual identity of the magazine as his Hungarian predecessor Martin Munkácsi had been to the American edition, with his work appearing in almost every single issue of *Bazaar* until the end of 1960.

In terms of both fashion and its photography, Kublin's era was a revolutionary one. Dior's 1947 'Corolle' collection (famously dubbed 'The New Look' by Carmel Snow) had launched the golden age of couture: fashion as an art form that few could afford but everyone could admire in the pages of a magazine. But it was interpreted to very different effect by Kublin and his famous contemporaries at *Bazaar*, such as Richard Avedon, Hiro and Lillian Bassman. Avedon's models did not allow the formality of the clothes they wore to interfere with their postwar freedoms. They were not austerely aloof, but twirled, jumped, ran and roller-skated on the streets (often to the visible consternation of passers-by), filled with the joy of their youth and the fun of fashion. To the reader, Avedon's photographs seemed to be moments snatched from a life – they made no attempt to be careful portrayals of clothes. Hiro was a master technician whose work played with surrealism and optical illusion; Lillian Bassman's experimentation took the form of playing with techniques when creating her delicate, feminine take on fashion imagery, hand-painting onto gelatin silver prints or removing an element of the camera lens to produce a soft-focus effect.

In contrast, Kublin's fashion photography was intended to highlight the craft of the couturier rather than his own, and he shied away from adopting the dynamic and naturalistic techniques that had become popular. His models remained formal in their perfection, carefully posed, and – aside from the shots of his partner and muse Katinka Bleeker – were not so much the focus of his gaze as their attire. They were usually shot in a studio and lit to allow every detail of the garment's shape and design to be seen. This was a skill Kublin had honed to perfection working for Balenciaga's archives, where his photographs were as practical in their purpose as they could be evocative in execution, intended as they were to record the detail of each design, and to discourage piracy, which was a perennial and widespread problem. Kublin was also recruited to work for Yves Saint Laurent – who became a friend – as well as Givenchy, Dior and Chanel.

By the spring of 1959, Kublin's work had crossed the Atlantic, and his byline began appearing in the American edition of *Bazaar*, under the aegis of its new art director Henry Wolf, who had taken over from the iconic Alexey Brodovitch. Kublin had arrived at a turning point for the magazine, much as it had been in 1951 for the British edition. Now, *Bazaar's* famous old guard – Snow, Brodovitch and Vreeland – had moved on, the era of couture was giving way to ready-to-wear, and to be young was everything; yet Kublin's work remained posed, formal and architectural. It was in this period that Gian Paolo Barbieri worked for him briefly as an assistant. In a recent interview, Barbieri recalled arriving to meet Kublin in Paris, dressed in his best blue

jacket and tortoiseshell glasses. 'He immediately told me that I was never to show up dressed like that again and that I was on trial for two days,' he told *i-D* magazine (February 2023). 'They were the hardest days of my life; during this time, however, I learnt everything about photography and fashion.' Barbieri, of course, went on to become one of the most acclaimed names in fashion photography, while his teacher, by contrast, remains relatively unknown, even today. The reason must be a matter of timing. Kublin died suddenly in 1966, missing out on the explosion of interest in fashion photography that saw it recast as fine art and worthy of exhibiting in galleries and museums, while his colleagues such as Penn and Avedon went on to have lengthy careers.

It is tantalising to speculate how Kublin's work would have developed during the seismic societal shifts of the late 1960s and 1970s. But whether it would have reflected them, or whether, perhaps, his experiences as a wartime photographer had left him with an enduring determination to offer the viewer an elegant refuge from turmoil and chaos, we will never know.

THOMAS KUBLIN

PHOTOGRAPHIES ET ILLUSTRATIONS

RIC. 31-21   45, RUE SAINTE-ANNE
RIC. 31-93   PARIS - 1ᴱᴿ

The Abraham Textile Archive is now part of the Swiss National Museum in Zurich. Among the objects in this collection are fashion photographs, including work by Tom Kublin. Kublin took hundreds of photos for Abraham as part of the company director Gustav Zumsteg's pursuit to build a visual portfolio showcasing haute couture designs made with its luxury fabrics. Tom Kublin was the photographer from 1953 through 1966, and he captured models wearing Abraham silk garments by many designers, including, most frequently, by Cristóbal Balenciaga.

1953, Abraham Textile Archive   37

1954, Abraham Textile Archive

1955, Abraham Textile Archive   45

48   1957, Abraham Textile Archive

52   1957, Abraham Textile Archive

1957, Abraham Textile Archive

1957, Abraham Textile Archive

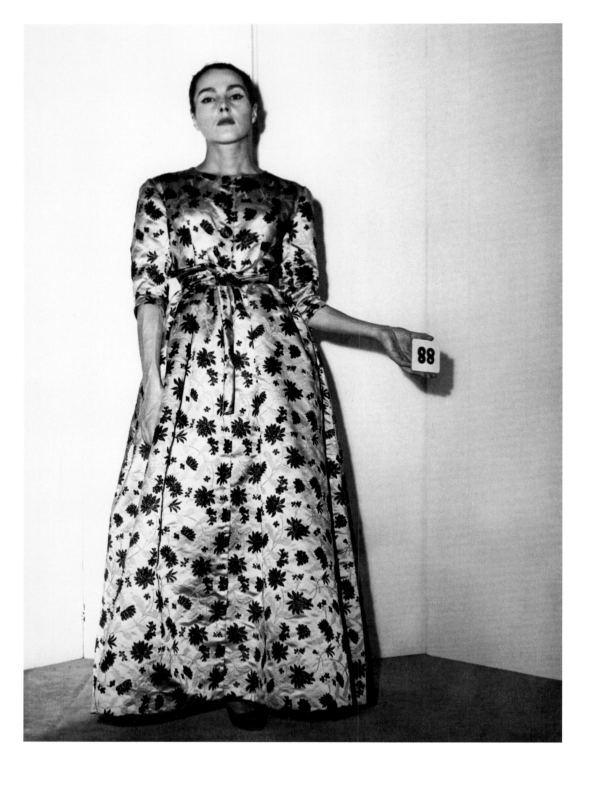

The images in this book captioned 'Balenciaga Archives Paris' are photographs taken by Tom Kublin from 1955 through 1966 for the House of Balenciaga. Most couture houses at this time relied heavily on licence sales – each season, designs were licensed to international clients to be replicated and sold in luxury stores around the world – but the illegal production of copycat garments was a real threat to business, and producing a complete photographic record of every look in a collection was how a house recorded copyright in its original couture designs. The models in these archive photographs hold cards (or sometimes they are propped on the floor) bearing reference numbers unique to the looks they are wearing.

1957, Balenciaga Archives Paris

HARPER'S
Bazaar

Winter Sports: Where to Go, What to Wear

Alice B. Toklas on Cooking with Champagne

How to be Liked, How to be Loved

December 1957
Three Shillings & Sixpence

HARPER'S BAZAAR
May 1957

● This season, designers—English
and French—point down
not one but several highways of
fashion: the fruits of their
entente cordiale, the new clothes
with all their throwaway
elegance waiting for you in the shops.
What this issue does is to
put up some signposts along the
summer's way. The path
you take is up to you: blowaway or
belted, fluent or full, impose
your own outline on the affable
alternatives. Remember,
before you plunge, that the
silhouette gives only part of the
picture: the fabric has never been
more important. Look, then,
for the eye-deceiving softness of
wool like silk, of cotton
like wool; for the nostalgic names—
georgette, charmeuse; for
something chiffon and something
blue; and the deep freeze
of summer white . . . Remember,
finally, that a felicitous
accessory is the yeast in fashion—and
the glittering, the incomparable
accessory is jewellery.
Right: the brilliance in the diamond
sparkle—necklace and
earrings by Van Cleef & Arpels.
The surprise in the head-
dress—two black roses
on a ribbon band. Balenciaga.

PHOTOGRAPH BY KUBLIN

Tom Kublin worked on assignment for a number of magazines and
from 1954 became a favoured photographer for the British edition
of the fashion monthly *Harper's Bazaar*. He worked on reports, features
and cover shoots under the editorship of Eileen Dickson.

1958, Abraham Textile Archive

1958, Abraham Textile Archive

1958, Abraham Textile Archive

1958, Balenciaga Archives Paris

1958, Balenciaga Archives Paris

1958, Balenciaga Archives Paris   83

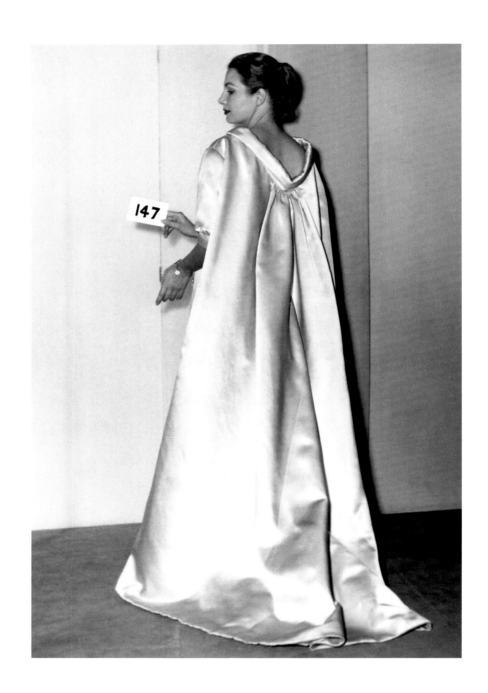

1958, Balenciaga Archives Paris

88   1958, Balenciaga Archives Paris

HARPER'S
Bazaar

The
HB
Your Look *for Now*

NOVEMBER 1958   Three Shillings and Sixpence

1958, Abraham Textile Archive

1959, Abraham Textile Archive

1959, Abraham Textile Archive

1960, Abraham Textile Archive

1960, Abraham Textile Archive

Town & Country is an American lifestyle magazine owned, like *Harper's Bazaar*, by the Hearst media group. It enjoyed a similarly elite readership, keen for the latest trends from Paris. From the early 1960s the magazine featured advertisements, shot by Tom Kublin, for licensed Balenciaga garments available to buy in renowned department stores in the US.

November 1960, *Town & Country*

FIRST AND LAST WORD IN FASHION

HARPER'S
BAZAAR

JUNE 1960 · 3/6

THIS
SPARKLING
SUMMER

FASHION IN
ACCESSORIES

BEAUTY:
THE LOOK
FOR WHITE

PARTY SETTINGS:
COLOUR DESIGNS BY
CARL TOMS

ROBIN DOUGLAS-HOME writes on
THE SEASON TODAY—FROLIC OR RAT-RACE?

From 1953, Tom Kublin's work featured in the French monthly fashion magazine *Jardin des Modes*, one of the main publications that contributed to the dissemination of French couture after the Second World War.

November 1960, *Jardin des Modes*

1961, Balenciaga Archives Paris

135

1961, Balenciaga Archives Paris

May 1961, *Jardin des Modes*

1961, Abraham Textile Archive

1961, Balenciaga Archives Paris

　　　　1962, Abraham Textile Archive

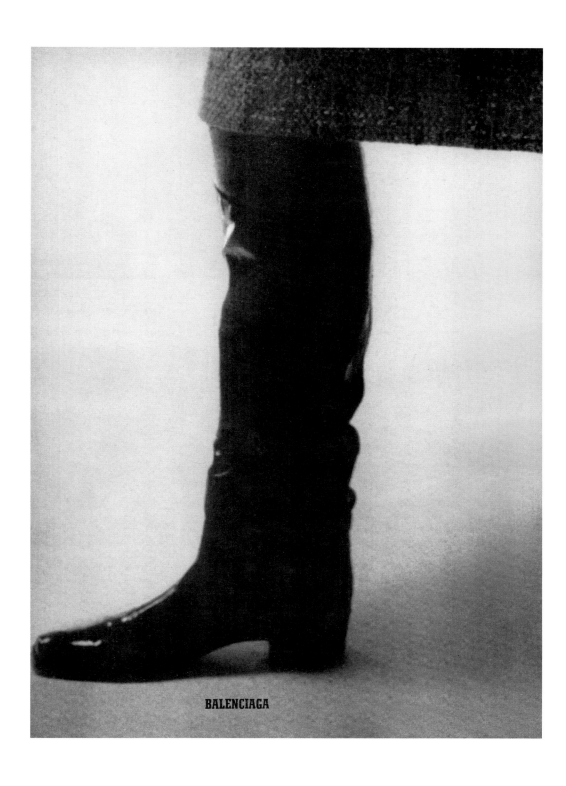

BALENCIAGA

HARPER'S

BAZAAR

JULY 1962 60c

Clothes with
a Great Future

25 Years of
Balenciaga

Lady Sailor's
Diet

New Beauty Box

James Agee
Four Letters

Tom Kublin's photo for the story '25 Years of Balenciaga' graced the cover of the July 1962 issue of *Harper's Bazaar* US; he had been working for the American publication since 1959, with five years already under his belt on assignment for the British edition. American readers would have been able to purchase licensed copies of the Balenciaga designs they saw reported in *Bazaar* at high-end department stores such as Bergdorf Goodman, Macy's, Ohrbach's and Bloomingdale's.

novembre 1962 · 2,50 nf

began recording moving footage
is film, his camera was set up in the
n real time the models walking the
ks; each model takes a turn up and
g at the end to remove a coat or outer
the dress beneath. The show lasted

1963, Balenciaga on film

1963, Abraham Textile Archive

jardin DES Modes

Mai 1963
F 2,50

Balenciaga
et
Givenchy
Toutes les
robes
de l'été

N° 497 — publication mensuelle imprimée en france — allemagne : d/m. 4 — belgique : fr. b. 40 — espagne : pesetas 40 — grande-bretagne . 3/° — italie : lire 500 — suisse : fr. ° 3,50

1963, Abraham Textile Archive   143

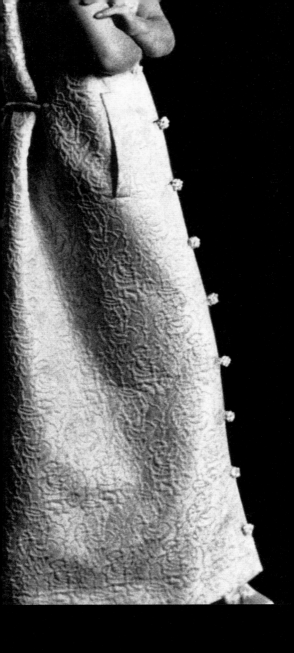

Fashion houses put on
also for department-st
replicas of original hau
affordable prices. Balen
American department s

1963 film still, Balenci

1964, Abraham Textile Archive

BALENCIAGA
Hiver 1964/65

Tom Kublin's partner in fashion and in life, the model Katinka Bleeker, appears wearing Balenciaga designs in a number of photographs that are now in the collection of the couple's only daughter, Maria Kublin. The photographs were originally intended for publication, but they endure as testimony to the intense creative relationship between Tom and Katinka.

1965, Collection Maria Kublin

1965, Collection Maria Kublin

1965, Balenciaga Archives Paris

1965, Collection Maria Kublin

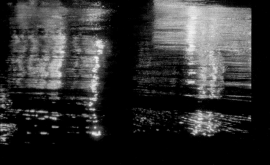  

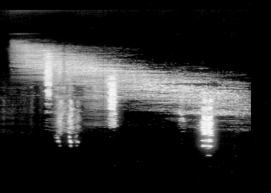  

In the decades after the Second World War, entering the perfume business was a way for French fashion houses to diversify their incomes and seek to mitigate the impact of declining haute couture sales. Balenciaga was no exception in this strategy and in 1947 he launched his first perfume 'Le Dix' followed by 'La Fuite des Heures' in 1948 and 'Quadrille' in 1955. With Katinka Bleeker as the model, Tom Kublin created this film commercial for Balenciaga's perfumes in 1965.

1965, Collection Maria Kublin

Tom Kublin's colour photographs illustrated the 24 September 1965 issue of this British newspaper supplement, with the feature announcing the launch of licensed Balenciaga designs on sale in London: 'twelve of Balenciaga's 1965 models go on show in Harrod's for the first time this week, and copies of them are on sale there... Now girls whose wishes turn to Paris will have not so far to travel.'

September 1965, *The Weekend Telegraph*

Tom Kublin's film for the Balenciaga Spring/Summer 1966 collection marks an artistic departure from his previous footage; firstly, it is shot in colour, and secondly, the models are directed and choreographed, twirling in and around one another wearing different looks, masterfully edited together and set to music that changes as the film moves from daywear into eveningwear.

1966, Balenciaga on film

1966, Abraham Textile Archive

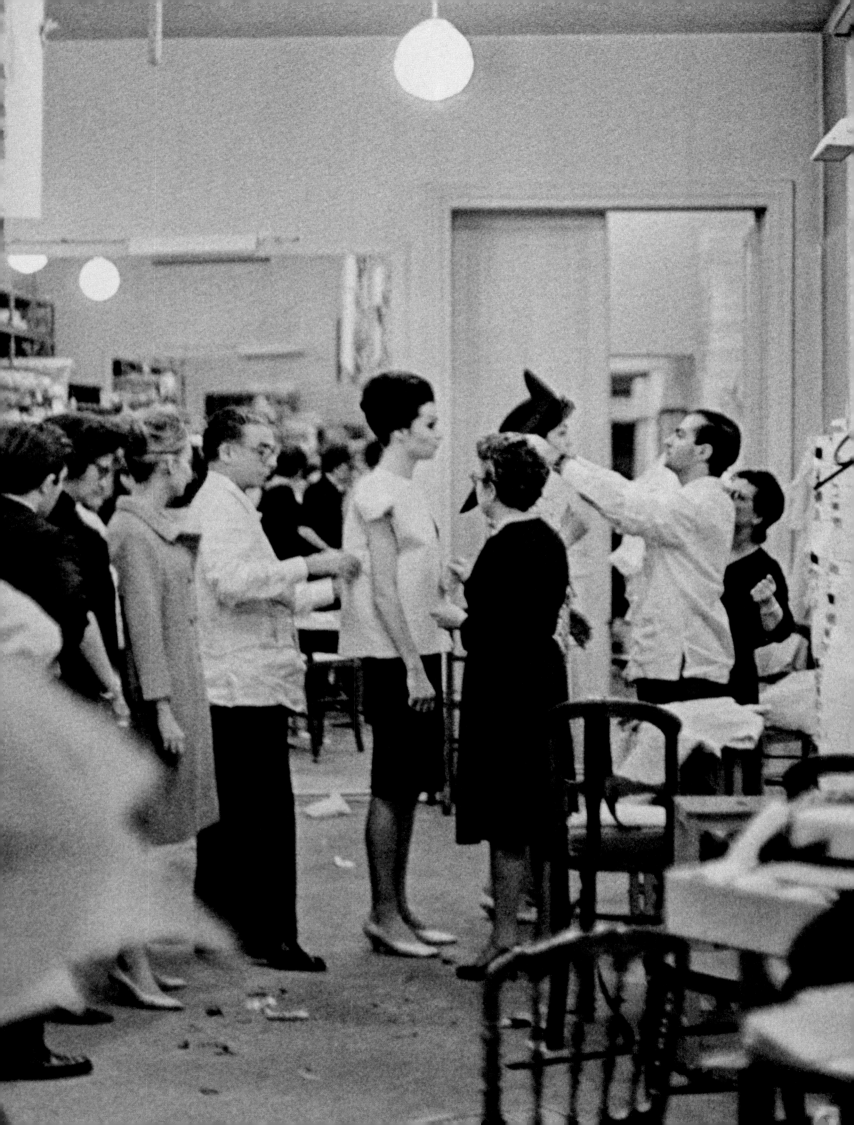

Film footage by Tom Kublin shows Cristóbal Balenciaga at work with
his team backstage. Wearing a white work jacket, Balenciaga makes
final adjustments to garments on models.

1966, Balenciaga on film

1966, Balenciaga on film

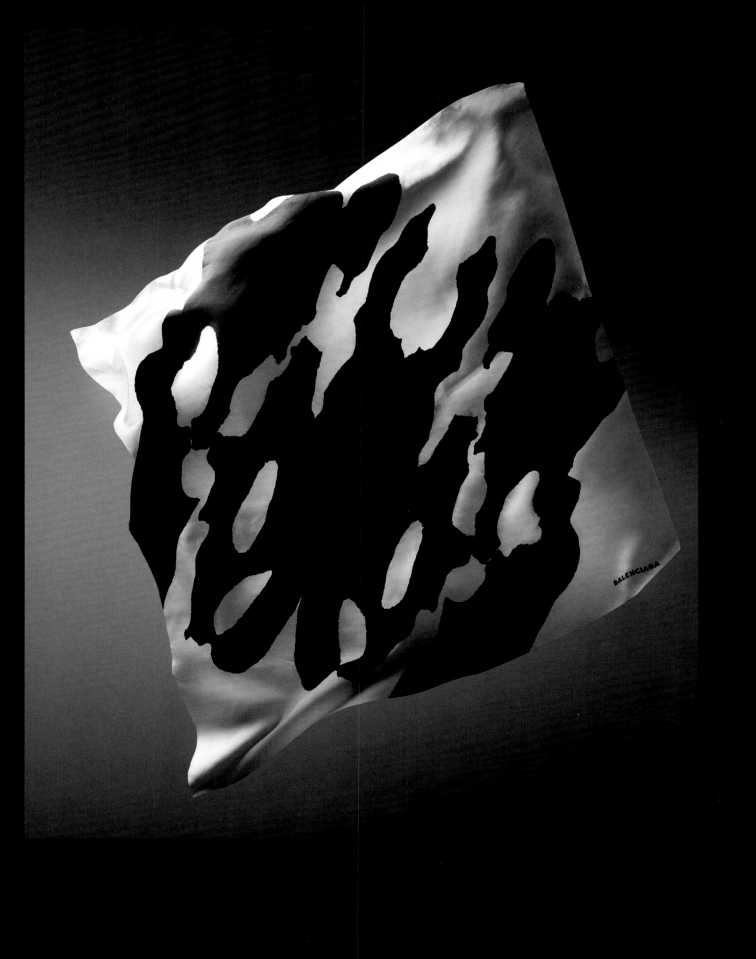

Silk scarf by Tom Kublin for Balenciaga. Kublin's design referenced black-and-white photography.

1. Hokky-Salla, Marianne, *The Esterházy Palace at Fertod* (Budapest: Corvina Kiado, 1979).
2. *Fotoélet*, vol. XIV, March 1944, 52.
3. A selection of these photographs appears in Tamási Miklós and Ungváry Krisztián, *Budapest 1945* (Budapest: Corvina, 2006).
4. 'They covered the collections', *Harper's Bazaar* UK, October 1954, 123.
5. *Der Bund*, vol. 98, no. 588, 17 December 1947 (2); *Engadiner Post*, vol. 57, no. 124, 26 October 1948.
6. 'Thomas Kublin, Famed Fashion Lensman is Dead', **Women's Wear Daily**, 1 June 1966, 46.
7. *Jardin des Modes,* June 1953, 1; October 1953, 1, 3, 4, 9, 10, 11, 14, 15; December 1953 (Noël edition), cover.
8. 'They covered the collections', *Harper's Bazaar* UK, October 1954, 122–23.
9. 'Thomas Kublin', *Harper's Bazaar* Germany, August 1966, 7.
10. *Der Bund*, vol. 103, no. 146, 27 March 1952; *Annabelle*, May 1952, cover; *Textiles Suisses*, 1952, 50.
11. The Balenciaga couture house sourced fabric from Abraham before the Second World War, as evidenced by the photograph of the suit published in *Textiles Suisses* (English edition), vol. 1942, 35.
12. Pallmert, Sigrid, 'The Abraham Archive: more than the sum of its parts!', *Soie Pirate* (Zurich: Scheidegger, 2010), 64–69.
13. Letter from the house of Balenciaga in Paris to Abraham, confirming that Mr Balenciaga would see, without any commitment, the company's collection for the following spring. Letter dated 29 September 1952, Abraham Textile Archive, Swiss National Museum, Zurich.
14. Angeletti, Norberto and Oliva, Alberto, *In Vogue: The Illustrated History of the World's Most Famous Fashion Magazine* (New York: Rizzoli, 2006), 48.
15. Hall-Duncan, Nancy, *The History of Fashion Photography* (New York: Alpine Book Company, 1979), 161.
16. Breward, Christopher, 'Intoxicated with images. The visual culture of couture', *The Golden Age of Couture: Paris and London, 1947–1957*, ed. Claire Wilcox (London: V&A, 2007), 192–99.
17. Many of the Parisian haute couture designers, but not Balenciaga, used to enter these kinds of photographs of their creations onto the *Register of Designs and Models*.
18. Miller, Lesley Ellis, *Balenciaga: Shaping Fashion* (London: V&A, 2017), 120–21.

19. *New York Herald Tribune*, 2 August 1956, 1 August 1957, 3 March 1958, cited in Pamela Golbin, *Balenciaga Paris* (London: Thames & Hudson, 2006), 104, 108, 111.
20. Balda, Ana, 'Balenciaga: Addressing misconceptions concerning his fashion press policies', *International Journal of Fashion Studies*, vol. 9 (2), April 2022, 81–82.
21. Balenciaga sold the licence for the feather evening dress on p. 163 of this book to Ohrbach's: 'They're curious about Ohrbach's copies', *The New York Times*, 9 September 1966, 77.
22. *Harper's Bazaar* UK, October 1957, 110–15.
23. Hubert de Givenchy in a letter to Ana Balda, 8 February 2012.
24. Katinka Bleeker, in-person interview with Maria Kublin, Amsterdam, 15 December 2022.
25. Widmer, Martin and Koellreuter, Isabel, 'From Abraham to Zumsteg', *Soie Pirate* (Zurich: Scheidegger, 2010), 35.
26. A photograph of Gustav Zumsteg with Cristóbal Balenciaga and Coco Chanel at the Kronenhalle appears in Marie Andrée Jouve and Jacqueline Demornex, *Balenciaga* (London: Thames & Hudson, 1989), 98.
27. Barbieri, Gian Paolo, 'Letter for Tom', 12 February 2019; pp. 27–28 of this book.
28. 'Chagall at the Louvre', *Harper's Bazaar* UK, October 1959, 130; 'Van Dongen's rise to fame', *Harper's Bazaar* UK, August 1960, 59.
29. 'Chagall at the Louvre', *Harper's Bazaar* UK, October 1959, 130.
30. *Cristóbal Balenciaga Museoa* (San Sebastián: Nerea, 2011), 64.
31. 'Thomas Kublin, Famed Fashion Lensman is Dead', *Women's Wear Daily*, 1 June 1966, 46; Maria Kublin has kept a silk Balenciaga handkerchief (pictured opposite) with a print that Katinka believes is one of the designs produced by Kublin for Abraham.
32. 'The Paris 1961 Look Spring and Summer', *Town & Country*, April 1961, 90–97.
33. Willie Landels, in-person interview with Maria Kublin, London, 29 November 2022.
34. 'Balenciaga. A new dimension by night', *Harper's Bazaar* UK, October 1958, 99.
35. The original painting has been held in Berlin's Gemäldegalerie collection since 1830.
36. 'Young talent above the crowd', *Harper's Bazaar* UK, June 1959, 54.
37. Katinka Bleeker, in-person interview with Maria Kublin, Amsterdam, 15 December 2022.

38. Katinka Bleeker, in-person interview with Maria Kublin, Amsterdam, 15 December 2022.
39. 'Balenciaga and la vie d'un chien', *The Times*, 3 August 1971, 6.
40. 'Balenciaga and Givenchy: Pacesetters of Paris', *The New York Times,* 16 September 1963, 46; 'Copies of Couture Imports Include Many Outstanding Buys', *The New York Times*, 13 March 1964, 36; 'Paris Look Is Feminine At Bergdorf', *The New York Times,* 8 March 1966, 31.
41. This commercial has been restored thanks to the Cristóbal Balenciaga Museum. The restored and digitized version was broadcast at the museum as part of the exhibition 'Tom Kublin for Balenciaga: An Unusual Collaboration', June–November 2022.
42. 'Thomas Kublin, Famed Fashion Lensman is Dead', *Women's Wear Daily*, 1 June 1966, 46.
43. Fellow photographer Jean Kublin took over from his brother Tom in his assignments for these houses.
44. 'The Harper's Bazaar Look: Starred in the Harper's Bazaar Look', *Harper's Bazaar* UK, November 1959, 58; 'Balenciaga', *Harper's Bazaar* UK, October 1957, 110; 'Happy encounter: Margot Fontaine', *Harper's Bazaar* UK, July 1965, 94–95; 'Van Dongen's return to fame', *Harper's Bazaar* UK, August 1960, 59; 'Chagall at the Louvre', *Harper's Bazaar* UK, October 1959, 131.
45. 'Ombres et mirages', *L'Impartial*, 13 December 1967, 25.

Ana Balda is a lecturer in Fashion History and Illustration and Fashion Photography at the School of Communication, University of Navarra, Spain. Her research covers the life and work of Cristóbal Balenciaga and the business side of haute couture, and she has published several journal articles and curated exhibitions on the subject. She also collaborates with the Cristóbal Balenciaga Museum.

Maria Kublin is the daughter of Tom Kublin and Katinka Bleeker. She works as an independent photography curator with a focus on fashion and fine art, and she is an editor for *Mirror Mirror Magazine*. Maria and Ana Balda co-curated the 2022 exhibition 'Tom Kublin for Balenciaga: An Unusual Collaboration' at the Cristóbal Balenciaga Museum.

Miren Vives is Director of the Cristóbal Balenciaga Museum, an institution which aims to preserve and disseminate Balenciaga's work, values and legacy from his birthplace of Getaria, Spain.

Katinka Bleeker is a former Miss Holland, fashion model and muse. During her career, Katinka worked with many top photographers, including Richard Avedon and Helmut Newton, but it was with Tom Kublin that she felt her role as a model became much more interesting. 'We had this connection and were aiming for the same: creating art', is how she describes their collaboration.

Gian Paolo Barbieri, born in Milan in 1935, began his photography career in his family's textile warehouse. In the 1960s he refined his craft under the guidance of Tom Kublin in Paris, an experience that shaped his distinctive photographic style. Barbieri caught the attention of the international fashion elite: his commercial campaigns have defined the creative voices of fashion giants including Walter Albini, Versace, Valentino and Yves Saint Laurent, and his photographs have appeared in the most important fashion magazines around the world. Today, Barbieri's works are showcased in esteemed international collections: the V&A Museum and the National Portrait Gallery in London, the Kunstforum in Vienna, the Musée du Quai Branly and the Pinault Collection in Paris, the NEC Collection in Zug and the MAMM in Moscow, to name just a few. In 2017, Barbieri established his foundation with the mission to preserve and promote his archive and works. In addition, Barbieri is represented by the 29 ARTS IN PROGRESS gallery in Milan.

Lydia Slater is the Editor-in-Chief of *Harper's Bazaar* UK. Prior to taking over, she launched *The Week's Fashion* magazine, edited the *Sunday Times Style* magazine and wrote regularly as an interviewer and a columnist for national newspapers including *The Times* and the *Daily Telegraph*. She sits on the advisory council of the Walpole, the official sector body for British luxury, and is a Fellow of the Royal Society of Arts.

PICTURE CREDITS

ACKNOWLEDGMENTS

Ana Balda

I am sincerely grateful to Maria Kublin for contacting me back in 2019, a connection that began the adventure of the exhibition 'Tom Kublin for Balenciaga: An Unusual Collaboration' and the publication of this book.

Thanks to Miren Vives for believing in the project and to her team for being one hundred percent involved. Exhibitions end and can be forgotten if they are not accompanied by a publication; and there is no publication without the support of a publisher. For this reason, I especially want to thank Adélia Sabatini for taking on this book and its promotion, and for seeing that without it, the work of Tom Kublin would remain little known. Thanks also to the team at Thames & Hudson: Jasmine Burville, Jane Cutter, Yasmin Garcha, Curtis Garner and Harriet Clarke, and the designers Stinsensqueeze. It has been a real pleasure working with you.

Maria Kublin

I wish to thank my co-curator and co-author, Dr. Ana Balda, for all her hard work, knowledge and positive energy. Thanks to everyone at Thames & Hudson for the opportunity to create this book. Special thanks to Adélia Sabatini, Commissioning Editor, for her support.

I am extremely grateful for the contribution by Lydia Slater, who has written such a wonderful text, despite an extremely busy schedule. I would like to extend my sincere thanks to Miren Vives and her amazing team at the Cristóbal Balenciaga Museum, who showed support from day one and helped to make the exhibition a success. I wish to show gratitude to Gian Paolo Barbieri for his warm welcome at his studio in Milan, and for giving me the opportunity to hold an interview. A special thanks to the late Willie Landels, founder of *Harper's & Queen* and designer, for sharing his personal memories of my father. And thank you to Patricia and Maurits, for all their help.

To my dear mother Katinka, who is one of the strongest women I know. I have only love and admiration. To my beautiful, adventurous and fierce daughter Eva Luna, for her patience and support. I love you beyond words. And in memory of my father, Tom Kublin.

The authors jointly wish to thank all those whose contributions made possible the exhibition, and therefore this book:

Gaspard de Massé, curator of the Balenciaga Archives Paris; Perrine Scherrer, photo editor of the Dior archive; Nathalie Vidal, responsible for the Hermès archives; Andrea Franzen, curator at the Swiss National Museum; Péter Baki, director of The Hungarian Museum of Photography; the Hungarian National Museum; the Musée des Arts Décoratifs; Julen Morras Azpiazu; Fondo Roger-Viollet; *Annabelle* magazine; Zoltán Fejér for his valuable knowledge; Maurits and Patricia for their neverending support; Baptiste Olivier for his beautiful photograph of the scarf designed by Tom Kublin; and Karin Kato, photo researcher at *Harper's Bazaar* US.

On the front cover
Photograph by Tom Kublin, 1962, Balenciaga Archives Paris

First published in the United Kingdom in 2024 by
Thames & Hudson Ltd, 181A High Holborn, London WC1V 7QX

First published in the United States of America in 2024 by
Thames & Hudson Inc., 500 Fifth Avenue, New York, New York 10110

Balenciaga – Kublin: A Fashion Record © 2024
Thames & Hudson Ltd, London

Designed by Stinsensqueeze

British Library Cataloguing-in-Publication Data
A catalogue record for this book is available from the British Library

ISBN 978-0-500-02653-3

Printed and bound in China by Artron Art (Group) Co., Ltd

Be the first to know about our new releases,
exclusive content and author events by visiting
thamesandhudson.com
thamesandhudsonusa.com
thamesandhudson.com.au